*To my husband
(of course)*

Acknowledgements

SPECIAL THANKS to my husband, Bob Lubin, who gave me inspiration and support. To my parents, Jakob and Rhaya Gil, for their loving model. To Ruth Failer, who encouraged me and supported me from the beginning. To Joan Morvay for her invaluable help.

Introduction

TRYING TO GIVE MY PARTNER original gifts for his birthday and to make this private holiday a special one is my reason for writing this book. I have learned that it doesn't matter how long you have been together, it's the extra attention of your gift giving that says "you are always on my mind."

This book contains more than 101 gift ideas that can be used for any occasion. Some of the gifts are humorous, some of them are intimate. All of them show how much you care.

It's not what you buy, or even how much you spend that makes a gift special. It's what you put into it—your thoughts, your planning, and your love.

Be creative, personal, and original. Make his gift something he will remember forever. No matter how "tough and strong" your partner may be, some of these gifts will bring tears to his eyes and a loving smile to his face. It will refresh and revitalize your relationship. A few of these gifts can even turn a previously ordinary evening into a mini-honeymoon!

Show Him Your Love will give you many creative gift ideas and original ways to present them. Some of these ideas are perfect for Father's Day, Valentine's Day, Anniversaries—or for a "just because" any time!

How To Use This Book

IN LOOKING FOR A GIFT IDEA from this book, you can simply pick an idea you like and present it exactly as it appears on the page, or you can personalize it. Choose the parts of the idea that suit your purpose best, and alter the rest with your own personal style. I suggest reading the book from cover to cover so you will be able to also mix and match ideas in your own unique way.

It is really a simple process. Let's look at a possible example. If the "Retirement" gift in Chapter Two really appeals to you but you want to do a little more, combine it with the "Retirement Gift II," from Chapter Four. You may even want to consider one of the ideas in Chapter Seven, "More Than One Gift."

Don't be afraid to use your imagination when creating your special gift. It will personalize the gift you will be proud to give.

For more alternatives, look for the Tips, Choices, and Options at the end of each gift idea. Also look at Chapters Nine and Ten for many more ideas for gifts and creative gift presentation.

Being creative and unpredictable with your gifts is what this book is all about.

Contents

Acknowledgments v
Introduction vii
How To Use This Book ix

ONE **Popular Gifts** 1
It's Only a Tie 2
Tie and Handkerchief 3
Matching Tie And ...? 4
Bathrobe 5
Bath Wrap 6
Cold - Warm - Hot 7
Dapper Partner 8
Wedding Ring Chain 9
Security Bracelets 10
Car Keychain 11
Gold Package (for his car) 12
Car Phone 13
Car Wash 14
Briefcase 15
New Business Card Case 16
On Your Birthday 17
It's Only a T-Shirt 18
Dogs are a Man's Best Friend 19

TWO	**Personal Gifts to Remember**	21
	Personal Messages	22
	Congratulation Video	23
	Audio Tape Souvenir	24
	Coin from His Birth Year	25
	Thanks for Being Born	26
	Birth Year Book	27
	First Happy Birthday	28
	Tree of Life	29
	Back to His Roots	30
	Retirement Card	31
	Trophy	32
	Playboy	33
	Traveling Present	34
	Home Is Where Love Is	35
	Handmade Scarf	36
	Gift from the Heart	37
THREE	**Add More to a Simple Gift**	39
	Bookmark	40
	Bookmark, Too!	41
	Pen & Paper	42
	Book Lover	43
	Old Record	44
	Movie Night	45
	Country Music Fan	46
	Cookie Jar	47
	Coffee Lover	48
	The Beach Boy	49
	New Sports Jacket	50
	New Wallet	51
	Hershey's Kisses	52
	Manicure & Pedicure	53

FOUR	**Sports Fan** 55
	Road Trip! 56
	Birthday with Friends 57
	The Golfer 58
	Retirement Gift II 59
	"Business" Towel 60
	Gift Certificate 61
	Exercise Room 62
	The Investor 63
	His Sport Hero 64
	Mini Television 65

FIVE	**Cakes, Dinners, and Flowers** 67
	A Piece of Cake 68
	No Big Deal! Birthday Cake 69
	The Box in the Birthday Cake 70
	Fortune Cookies 71
	Lunch for His Birthday 72
	Transport to Japan 73
	Dinner via Telegram 74
	Limo Ride to Dinner 75
	Surprise on the Bus 76
	Yourself as a Gift 77
	Birthday Flowers 78
	Roses to Make Him Blush! 79
	Roses 4 Him 80

SIX	**Paintings, Pictures, and Calendars** 83
	Emotional Gift 84
	Painted Picture 85
	Your Heart's on Canvas 86
	Action Pictures 87
	Signed Family Photo 88

Framed Item 89
Framed Cartoon 90
Your Song 91
A Birthday Card to Remember 92
His Private Calendar 93
One-Month Calendar 94
Appointment Calendar 95

SEVEN **More Than One Gift** 97
More Than One Gift, How 98
More Than One Gift, When 99
A Gift Each Hour 100
Seven-Day Gift 102
The Twelve Days of Christmas 104
A Gift for Each Year 106
Shabby Bag 107
Birthstones 108

EIGHT **When Money Is Not a Problem** 111
Talk Radio Fan 112
Country Music Vacation 113
Fishing Weekend 114
Forced Vacation 115
Father and Child 116
Surprise on a Cruise 117
Massage Chair 118
Someone Loves You 119
Musical Partner 120
Car on His Birthday 121

xiv *Show Him Your Love*

NINE	**For Lovers and Others**	123
	For Men Who Love "Toys"	124
	Office "Toys"	125
	Car "Toys"	126
	Sport Gifts	127
	"Just Because" Gifts	128
	For Lovers and Others	129
TEN	**Finally!**	131
	How to Find a "Bingo!"	132
	Creative Presentations	133
	Many Birthday Cards	135
	Cards, Cards, Cards	136
	Invitation to His Party	137
	Advertising	138
	Your Favorite Gift Ideas	139
	Afterword	141

― CHAPTER ONE ―

Popular Gifts

🌿🌿🌿

Ties, shirts, and books are common gift ideas,
yet you can still make them fun to give and receive.
The key is to make a unique presentation
with a touch of humor.
Your partner will laugh and enjoy these gifts,
and you will have fun giving them.

Gift Idea 1

IT'S ONLY A TIE

TO DRESS UP THE GIFT of a **tie,** purchase the tie as the main gift, toss in a shirt, and dress it up with the tie. The shirt does not have to be a new shirt; it can be a shirt from his closet. Add an old tie pin and cufflinks. Arrange them nicely in a gift box and present them as if they were all new. This presentation is guaranteed to make him laugh.

OPTION *An old suit is another funny idea for this gift.*

Gift Idea

2

TIE AND HANDKERCHIEF

ANOTHER WAY to give a simple gift of a tie is to buy the tie with a matching **handkerchief.** Monogram the tie and the handkerchief with his initials and the date of the event. This special presentation will make the tie different from any other tie you've given him.

TIP

*This is a good gift for a promotion,
an anniversary,
or a son's Bar Mitzvah or confirmation.*

Gift Idea
3

MATCHING TIE AND...?

MEN HAVE TRADITIONALLY BOUGHT WOMEN gifts of sexy matching lingerie that can make an evening fun when the two of you know what **underwear** you are wearing. Why can't this work for men too?

Today, department stores have underwear, silk boxer shorts, socks, ties, and suspenders that have the same patterns on them. Some of them are wild patterns with vivid colors, strange pictures, or even cartoon characters! If you can't find matching patterns, opt for a solid color. Tell your man that every time he wears that tie (or suspenders, socks, etc.) he must wear the matching underwear, too.

TIP
*Only you and
he will know
when and what
underwear
he wears.*

Gift Idea
4

BATHROBE

TO BRIGHTEN UP a purchase of a new **bathrobe** for your partner, have it monogrammed. The monogram does not just have to be his initials—it can be a cartoon, a picture, or an emblem. When your partner wakes up and wanders into the bathroom to shower, he will be surprised to see a brand new personalized bathrobe waiting for him.

Another way to present the robe is after a long day of work. Fill the bathroom with balloons and hang up his new robe in the middle of them. Just as your husband is wondering if you have forgotten his birthday, he will walk into the bathroom for a pleasant surprise. Draw a relaxing bubble bath for him to enjoy as he tries on his new robe.

OPTIONS

A silk bathrobe is a luxurious choice.

Attach some paper hearts to his new robe.

Gift Idea
5

BATH WRAP

THIS GIFT IS AN IDEAL GIFT TO REMEMBER a special beach holiday. Take a **beach towel** you used or bought on your vacation together and create a bath wrap. You can easily sew this wrap with some elastic and Velcro for the waist. If you are not in the mood to sew, this gift can still be easily made with double-sided tape that irons on.

When he gets out of the shower, hand him his new wrap! It is an original way for him to remember the wonderful time you had together. Won't he look great in this skirt!

OPTIONS

If you cannot sew, you can give the towel to a tailor to create the wrap.

When you don't have a memento towel, buy one with a crazy print on it.

Gift Idea
6

COLD - WARM - HOT

THIS FUN PRESENTATION IDEA came to a friend of mine after reading some of my ideas while I was writing this book.

This friend's husband loved brass objects, so for his birthday, she bought him a standing brass towel rack. She also bought new monogrammed towels, and adorned the rack with them, along with balloons and birthday cards.

When he came home from work, the entire family joined in the game of helping him find his birthday present. As he wandered through the house, they gave him clues of only "cold" if he was far from the present, "warm" if he was getting close to the present, and "hot" if he was very close to the present. With their help he soon found his birthday surprise.

TIP
To add more luxury to this gift, buy a heated towel stand to keep the towels warm and dry for after his bath.

Gift Idea
7

DAPPER PARTNER

IS YOUR PARTNER extremely well groomed and meticulous about the condition of his shoes? Is he always brushing his shoes to make sure that they are shiny? If you can answer yes to these questions, then the perfect gift for him is an electric shoe polisher. With this gift he won't have to take the time to sit down and take off his shoes to shine them. Every time he passes this gift, he can give those shoes a quick shine. Every man who wears shoes will be happy with a gift like this. Not only will he be able to shine his shoes himself, but each time that he does, he will be reminded of you.

> **TIP**
> *This gift can also be monogrammed with his name.*

Gift Idea
8

WEDDING RING CHAIN

IF YOUR PARTNER IS LIKE MINE and does not like to wear his wedding ring, or needs to remove it daily for work (surgeon, carpenter, plumber), you can buy him a simple gold or silver chain to put through the ring to wear around his neck.

If he does not like jewelry at all, buy a small keychain with an extra chain attached for the wedding ring. He will not have to wear the ring, but he will always have it in his pocket or car.

TIP

If you have not had his wedding ring inscribed, now would be a perfect time.

Gift Idea
9

SECURITY BRACELETS

WHEN SOMEONE YOU LOVE has a certain **medical condition** (allergic to penicillin, for example) and needs to wear a medical alert bracelet, you can customize a special gift for him. Have his medical alert bracelet created in gold or silver. Make sure you get all the information off his original bracelet so your jeweler can accurately engrave the new one. Have the jeweler engrave your partner's name and phone number on the back of the bracelet as well as a physician's name and phone number.

Not only is the gift more attractive than the traditional bracelets, but if he should need it, you may save his life.

OPTIONS

This gift also works well for medical alert charms on necklaces.

Simple styles of these bracelets are available at drug stores in stainless steel.

Gift Idea
10

CAR
KEYCHAIN

MANY YEARS AGO I HAD A PARTNER who had a Mercedes sports car. He loved this car so much he even had a **keychain** with the Mercedes symbol on it. While he was not using his car, I took the keychain to a jeweler and had it duplicated in gold. On his birthday I gave him the gold keychain, and was he surprised! He looked at his original keychain and then at the gold one I had just given him. I believe that, to this day, even though he doesn't have the Mercedes anymore, he still uses this gold keychain. If you have a partner who loves his car more than anything else, you know what to do.

TIP
Prepare for this gift with enough time before his birthday.

Gift Idea

11

GOLD PACKAGE
[FOR HIS CAR]

YOU CAN SURPRISE your partner by changing all of the chrome on his car to gold. (This gift can be expensive, depending on the type of car your partner owns.)

Take his car to the local dealership and ask the service department to install the gold package on his car. If you are on a budget, you can choose to have only a few items installed. For example, change all four door handles, or the steering wheel.

This can freshen up any old car or add something special to a new car. You should know by now if he loves his car, and if this would be a special gift for him.

TIP
You can add to this gift with a new seat cover, car mats, or anything else that will accessorize his car.

Gift Idea
12

CAR PHONE

DOES YOUR PARTNER NEED a new **portable phone** for his car? Replace his old phone with a new model with the same phone number. Have the new phone installed in his car. Decorate the outside of his car, and leave a long stemmed rose and a card inside next to the phone, so that when he gets into the car, he will notice the gift.

Or, you can buy him a cellular phone with one month of service prepaid. He can keep it in his glove compartment (for an emergency) or carry it with him wherever he goes. After a while, he will wonder how he ever survived without a portable phone.

REMEMBER
This is an expensive gift, one that a person usually buys for him or herself, so he will be especially surprised to find such a wonderful gift in his car.

Gift Idea
13

CAR WASH

SURPRISE YOUR PARTNER with a **gift certificate** to wash his car. You can give him as many certificates as you like. You can purchase them from your local car wash or a specialty detailing shop. There are even car wash services that will go to his home or office to wash his car.

Men are usually very proud of their cars and would appreciate a gift like this. It makes an especially nice gift for those men who are so busy that there isn't much time for them to wash their own car.

OPTIONS

If he ends up not wanting to use the gift for his own car, you can use it for yourself.

Gift Idea
14

BRIEFCASE

HE LOVES THAT OLD BRIEFCASE, but it definitely has seen better days! Take a good look at his **favorite briefcase** and start your search for a new one that looks exactly like it.

Early in the morning, place all of his paperwork from his old briefcase into the new one (make sure you don't leave anything inside!). Wrap the gift and hide it in the kitchen.

Make him a small breakfast party to celebrate his big day before he leaves for work. When he opens the gift, not only will he be surprised about the new briefcase, but he will be happy you saved him the extra time of transferring his paperwork.

CHOICES

You can do the same thing with an old favorite lunchbox.

Include new office toys inside the briefcase, if there is any room left.

Gift Idea
15

NEW BUSINESS CARD CASE

LOOK AT YOUR PARTNER'S BUSINESS CARDS and ask yourself if now is the time to create a **new look** for them. How much you have them changed depends on how well you know that he will want you to do this. You can change the black lettering to gold, or put a small logo in one corner of the card. Shop at your local print shop for more ideas.

After you have had the new cards printed, buy him a business card case with a silver or gold finish. If you can afford to have a jeweler set his birthstone in the case along with having his initials engraved, the finished product will be super!

CHOICES

Place a special message inside the card case cover.

Add note pads printed with the same design to the gift.

Reproduce his business card on a mug.

Gift Idea
16

ON YOUR BIRTHDAY

ON YOUR BIRTHDAY, show him it is more blessed to give than to receive! Surprise him with a **gift for him**. It is saying to him (without speaking), "You are important to me even on my special day!"

It doesn't have to be an expensive gift. A good idea would be to buy a plate or mug with the words, "You are special, today." You can also express your feelings on a big T-shirt, or buy matching night shirts made of silk or flannel for each of you. Two sports outfits would work well, too.

TIPS

Send his mom flowers as a "thank you" for the best gift she ever gave you (her son).

Make sure he doesn't get the feeling that you are reminding him to buy you a gift.

Gift Idea
17

IT'S ONLY A T-SHIRT

WHAT CAN BE FUNNIER and more unique than a **T-shirt with a photo of him** when he was a baby or teenager?

You can easily improve on this gift. You can make a different T-shirt for each of your family members: make him a shirt with his baby picture on it, make yourself one with a picture of when the two of you first met, and make shirts for your children with pictures of their father at their ages.

CHOICE

If you are planning a surprise birthday party, make T-shirts with his picture on them for all of the guests to wear to the party. Pick out as many photos as you can find.

Gift Idea

18

DOGS ARE A MAN'S BEST FRIEND

ONE DAY WHEN HE LEAST EXPECTS IT, surprise him. Buy him a **puppy** (try to find out his favorite kind) along with a card that promises to take care of his new pet while he is away. While you are at the pet store or humane society, be sure to buy some necessary dog accessories. These can include dog tags, a collar, dog food, a leash, and/or a pooper scooper.

If he already has a pet he loves, take a picture of it and have it enlarged to poster size. Make the gift from his pet by signing the card with a paw print. Remember, the more you love his pet, the more he will love you.

TIPS

This can be an especially touching gift if he has had a dog before.

When presenting the gift, tie a big helium balloon to the puppy with the words "Happy Birthday" or "I Love You!"

― Chapter Two ―

Personal Gifts to Remember

❦ ❦ ❦

Some gifts can become presents that
your partner will remember forever.
These are gifts that you took time to plan,
prepare, and participate in. These are gifts that
warm and strengthen your relationship.
These are gifts that say
"after all these years you are still in my heart and
Number One in my mind."

Gift Idea
19

PERSONAL MESSAGES

LET YOUR MAN KNOW HOW MUCH HE IS LOVED with personal **messages** from his friends and family. This is a wonderful gift; however, it requires a lot of time and planning. Buy a nicely made journal with blank pages. Make a list of names and addresses of your partner's good friends and family. Start the list with people who live overseas because it might take a while for them to receive mail. Call the first person on the list and tell them that you are sending the journal, and what page they should write their message on (be sure to number the pages in the book).

You may want to save the first few pages for your message and perhaps your children's. When you receive the journal back, call the next person on the list and repeat the process until you have gotten everyone to fill out a page.

Get a temporary post office box to have the journal sent to, because you do not want your partner to accidentally come across the gift before it is finished. Put his photo on the cover and present it to him on his special day.

TIPS

Give yourself at least a year to complete this gift.

You can add a table of contents.

Gift Idea
20

CONGRATULATION VIDEO

GIVE YOUR PARTNER A VIDEO OR CASSETTE TAPE of many of his **friends** wishing him a happy birthday. This is a unique gift that can be enjoyed over and over again.

Use a video camera to record a personal greeting or good wishes from his friends and family. (If you do not have a video camera, borrow or rent one.) Make sure you indicate that they should only talk for a certain amount of time—you don't want to run out of video tape! The more spontaneous these greetings are, the better, so no dress rehearsals! Videotape yourself last with a romantic message that he will remember.

Label the video: "Congratulations Video from All of Us Who Love You."

OPTIONS

If a video camera's cost is out of reach, record the greeting on an audio cassette tape. You can also record people over the phone who are too far away to videotape.

Remember, this gift also requires a lot of preparation and time.

Gift Idea 21

AUDIO TAPE SOUVENIR

WHEN YOU AND YOUR PARTNER HAVE A SONG that is "our song" or if you know certain songs that he absolutely loves, record these songs on a **gift tape** for him. Between the songs talk to him: read him poems that you like, tell him why the song is special to you, and don't be afraid to sing a little. There is nothing more special than being sung to. Put the tape in his car so it will play when he turns on his car to go to work. I gave this gift to my partner with some of his favorite songs on it. In between the songs I read to him a card that I had given him earlier in our relationship to remind him of that time. I sang along with the songs and said some very funny things.

TIPS

Choose songs from his favorite singer.

Remember to break off the safety pieces of the cassette tape so no one can record over it by accident.

To add to this gift, include a small Walkman tape player.

Gift Idea
22

COIN FROM HIS BIRTH YEAR

COINS, currently inexpensive, have the potential to turn into a **valuable investment** that can double as a unique gift idea especially for him.

Check at a local coin shop for a coin imprinted with the year of his birth. The prices of coins fluctuate daily, depending on the coin market. Avoid buying collector's coins that come in a special plastic case because, after you take the coin out of the case, its value drops significantly.

If you are unable to find the year you are looking for, buy him an antique gold coin, or a recently minted gold coin, and put it on a gold chain for him to wear. If you are on a budget, use a silver coin of any denomination and make it into a keychain for him.

TIP
If your partner likes to gamble a little, a collection of vintage casino chips is a special gift.

Gift Idea
23

THANKS FOR BEING BORN

THANK YOUR PARTNER for being born by **gathering things** from the year or day he was born. Some examples would be:

- His birth certificate.
- A copy of a magazine that was issued on the month and year of his birth.
- A copy of a daily newspaper printed on his birth date.
- A bottle of wine from the year he was born.
- His birth announcement.
- A video tape of the movie which won the academy award the year he was born.

Place all the "oldies but goodies" in a large gift box and add some humorous memorabilia from his childhood (old toys, clothes, or music) to make him laugh. Present the box to him with the words "Thanks for Being Born" on the outside.

TIPS

The library is a great resource for print media. Use their computers to conduct a search, or ask a librarian to assist you.

A Playboy or other men's magazine from his birth year can be an interesting idea.

Gift Idea
24

BIRTH YEAR BOOK

THERE IS AN INTERESTING BOOK that is currently available in most greeting card stores and large chain bookstores. It is a small booklet which contains news headlines, movies, sports highlights, and magazines from the year a person was born (a large number of years are available).

Don't just give your partner the booklet of his birth year—personalize it! Take apart the booklet by removing the staples, separate the pages, and add new ones with a picture of your partner the day he was born and a copy of his birth certificate.

When you have made the pages the way you want them to appear, take it to a copy center and have them enlarge and bind the pages to a HUGE size.

CHOICE
On the cover of the birth year book write,
"The most important thing that happened this
year was that (his name) was born."

Gift Idea
25

FIRST
HAPPY BIRTHDAY

IF LIFE HAS GIVEN YOUR PARTNER A SECOND CHANCE, or you want to make him feel young again, give him **his first birthday** all over again! Buy little baby toys that are given to a baby on its first birthday celebration, or fill up a baby bottle with his favorite adult drink.

Since these gifts are usually small, you can easily sneak them into a party, if your are having one, or you can make this first birthday an intimate moment between the two of you. These gifts will prove to be a very touching moment, so prepare carefully.

TIPS

A 50th birthday is a perfect occasion for this gift.

Be sure to get candles, hats, and plates with a baby theme.

Have a box of tissues ready.

Gift Idea
26

TREE OF LIFE

WHEN YOUR PARTNER STARTS TO FEEL OLD and ponder mid-life, remind him of **how special** he is to you and how much you love him.

Plant him a tree (a sapling or larger) in the yard which will bear fruit or flowers in the spring and summer. Dedicate a big plaque on the ground next to the tree saying, "A tree represents growth. It is the symbol of life" and that the tree has been planted in his honor.

The tree represents a new beginning of the rest of his life that he has yet to live.

OPTION

You can also plant rose bushes around the tree for a beautiful accent.

Gift Idea
27

BACK TO HIS ROOTS

SURPRISE HIM WITH TICKETS for a trip back to his **hometown**. Make reservations for the hotel and flight, and walk with him through his childhood.

When your partner's family are immigrants, make plans to take him back to his family's roots. Together, the two of you can visit the home country of his family.

When you are in his hometown, take plenty of pictures which can be used for future gifts. Visit the hospital where he was born, the elementary school he attended, the home in which he grew up, and the playground where he played. Walking through his childhood will be a very emotional and unforgettable experience for him.

TIPS

While you are in his hometown, place flowers on family members' graves.

Buy souvenirs for future gifts for him.

Pick up a few city maps for wrapping these gifts.

Gift Idea
28

RETIREMENT CARD

AFTER MANY YEARS of hard work your partner decides to retire. Surprise him with a special gift that he will use for many years to come. Have a personal business card designed and printed for him. That way, if someone asks for his number or his card, he does not have to fumble for a pen, or come up with lengthy explanations. He can simply pull out his card.

Subtle humor is good to use on cards for this purpose. Print a phrase such as "Happily retired," or "Not working for now." The cards will make him feel important (and save embarrassment), and he will know you are still thinking of him.

OPTIONS

If he has a favorite hobby, have it printed on the card ("Fisherman," or "Artist").

Combine this gift with some quality personalized stationery.

Gift Idea
29

TROPHY

IF YOUR PARTNER HAS NEVER RECEIVED RECOGNITION for a **personal accomplishment** in the way of a trophy or a medal, have one made for him! It can be for sports, carpentry, fathering, or for being a wonderful lover. Look for a nice trophy or medal at a sports store, and have it engraved with his accomplishment. Pop open a bottle of champagne to celebrate the occasion.

TIPS

This is a perfect gift for Father's Day. —— *Ask the store employees for help in making just the right trophy for you.*

Combine the trophy or medal gift with a framed diploma on the same subject.

Gift Idea
30

PLAYBOY

HE IS A SHY ONE, but you love him for it! Surprise him with some **Playboy underwear!** But don't stop there—make the gift even more intimate with some satin sheets and pillowcases. Sew on your own labels which read "With love from (your name)" or "Made especially for you by (your name)." Blank labels can be purchased at any fabric store.

Be careful with this gift—your man might start to think he is a real playboy! Trust him to use his gifts properly when you are not with him between those sheets!

TIPS

Make sure the Playboy products you buy are originals and not imitations—it makes a big difference!

Instead of using labels, you can embroider on the sheets, yourself.

Personal Gifts to Remember

Gift Idea
31

TRAVELING PRESENT

IF YOUR PARTNER IS GOING away on business or pleasure for the first time and doesn't have all of the necessary luggage, you can buy him all the **things he will need,** like a money belt, a travel bag, luggage, and luggage tags. For a special touch, have metal luggage tags made with his name and address engraved on them. Make everything ready for him by putting two tags on each bag.

If you want to remind him of you, include with this gift a map of the city where you live and circle your area or street. Provide him with paper and a stamped envelope with your address already filled out on it. Put everything in his suitcase so that he will find the gift when he arrives at his destination.

OPTIONS

Use the map of your city for wrapping paper.

Buy him a prepaid long distance calling card to take with him so he can keep in touch!

Gift Idea
32

HOME IS WHERE LOVE IS

IF YOUR PARTNER TRAVELS OFTEN and you would like to remind him of home, "where love is," here are a few gift ideas that you can use:

- Buy him a double wrist watch with two watches connected to each other. One of the watches should show the correct time at his "home, sweet home." This will help him remember the time to call home to his family. Engrave the back of the watch with words like, "Home is where love is."

- You can buy him an alarm clock or pocket watch as a second private watch, different from his wristwatch. Engrave it with the same special words.

- Purchase a pillow cover and embroider it with the words, "Home is where love is." Give this to him as a gift to use on his pillow, no matter where he is.

Gift Idea
33

HANDMADE SCARF

WHAT CAN SHOW YOUR LOVE MORE than creating a gift with your own hands? Make your partner a **scarf.** It is not difficult; all you have to do is learn one simple knitting stitch and repeat the stitch for as long as it takes to make the scarf as long as you want.

When you finish the scarf, you will be proud to present this handmade gift to your partner and he will be flattered to find out that you made the scarf especially for him with your own hands. Be sure to sew a label on the scarf that reads "Made with love from...."

TIPS

If you like the scarf idea, you can also make him a vest or tie.

Additional ideas are available in fabric, knitting, and craft stores.

Gift Idea
34

GIFT FROM THE HEART

AN INTIMATE GIFT THAT WILL ALWAYS BE TREASURED by your partner is to **put your feelings into words** and write them down on paper.

Sometimes the best ideas of what to write come at the wrong time. Don't let that happen to you. Carry a small tape recorder with you and record your notes wherever you may be— in the car, in the kitchen, in the bathtub. The spontaneity of this gift is part of what makes it so special. If you like to write, put your feelings on short notes, long notes, napkins, or even on your calendar. Express your feelings at any time of the day or night.

If you choose to use the tape recorder for this gift, rewrite your thoughts in a special book. You can also choose to rewrite these notes using calligraphy and give them to him wrapped in a nice box or glue them all into a blank book.

TIPS

Put the notes in a photo album.

You can add your own illustrations.

— Chapter Three —

Add
More to a Simple Gift

🌿🌿🌿

A gift does not have to be something extraordinary or expensive. However, when you give a gift, you want him to know you put more than just money into it. Your concerns, your thoughts, your humor, and your love will shine through. And all you did was add more to a simple gift.

In this chapter you will find ideas and details about how to add more to your gifts by making them special and imaginative.

Gift Idea
35

BOOKMARK

A BOOK IS A POPULAR GIFT IDEA. It is a gift that everyone likes to give and receive. When you want to make a book a little more special, combine it with a **personalized bookmark.** Not just any ordinary bookmark, but one that you make yourself from personal photos. To assemble the bookmark, take two pictures of your man and glue them back to back. (Make sure you use photos that will align well.) When the glue is dry, with a scissors cut the double-sided pictures into the size of a bookmark. Cut a small hole at the top and tie a colored ribbon through it. You may also laminate the bookmark in order to make it stronger.

Place your bookmark inside the book you will give. When he opens the book and sees this special bookmark, he will be sure to smile.

CHOICE
Instead of using pictures of him, you may consider pictures of something (or someone) that is very special to him.

Gift Idea
36

BOOKMARK, TOO!

ANOTHER TYPE OF PERSONALIZED BOOKMARK you can make yourself is a **"love-mark."** Write down as many reasons you can think of as to why you love him. Cut a piece of cardboard the size of a bookmark and cover it with all of these reasons. Use different colored inks or markers. Write in all directions: diagonal, up, down, crisscross, and crooked. Cover your entire gift with these special messages.

OPTIONS

Use a typewriter or computer to create your bookmark.

For another twist on the bookmark idea, put on some lipstick, and cover the bookmark with kisses.

Gift Idea
37

PEN & PAPER

HOW MANY TIMES have you given an elegant pen as a gift? This time, make it a little different. Order personalized **stationery and envelopes** with his name on top. You can do this inexpensively at most stationery stores or you can order through a mail-order catalog. Combine this with the pen and maybe an engraved letter-opener, and you have a unique gift with a personal accent. You can also combine the gift with a custom-made rubber address stamp with ink pad, or a personalized memo cube and stamp box.

EXTRAS

To make the gift even more special, have the pen engraved with his name or with a special message.

This is the perfect gift for Father's Day or as a graduation gift.

Gift Idea
38

BOOK LOVER

WHEN YOU KNOW your partner's **favorite author,** here is your opportunity to buy him a special gift. Buy him an assortment of books written by that author—but make sure they are not titles he already owns.

If you can find the author or publisher, see if you can send the books in to be autographed. If this is not possible, find a good book binder and have special leather covers made for the books. This may be a little expensive, but he will treasure these books for many years to come, especially if these book titles are important to him.

TIP
Add one of the personalized bookmark ideas from this book to make the gift extra-special!

Gift Idea 39

OLD RECORD

DO YOU KNOW your partner's **favorite song?** Maybe you both have a song that represents the early days when you first fell in love. Maybe that song was played at your wedding, or maybe it is a song from a movie that you both liked. Perhaps it is his favorite music from his high school days.

See if you can find an old record (a 78 or 45 rpm) of that special song. Create a special gift for him by making this record into a clock. If you prefer, you can have a watchmaker do the job for you.

This gift will look nice in his office or home.

TIPS

Look in thrift stores or flea markets for old records.

This gift can be used with the "More than One Gift" ideas in Chapter Seven.

You can use the record as a picture frame for a photo of the two of you.

Gift Idea
40

MOVIE NIGHT

GIVE A "MOVIE NIGHT" GIFT. If he admires a **specific actor or actress,** buy books, biographies, and memorabilia featuring that person. Rent or buy two or three movies with the actor or actress in the starring role. Combine these gifts with a director's chair with his name printed on the back.

It may be difficult to pack everything together. See if you can find a blanket or beach towel with a picture or title of one of his favorite movies, and wrap your presents inside of it. Top it all off with a copy of the script for the movie you are about to see (you can find most scripts in your local library or through a specialty mail-order catalog).

To make the gift simpler, instead of the director's chair, give a barrel of specialty popcorn or his favorite drink along with the movies.

TIP
Reserve the "movie night" idea for romantic movies.
Use your imagination!

Gift Idea
41

COUNTRY MUSIC FAN

IS YOUR PARTNER a **country music fan?** Create a tape of his favorite country music songs, or buy his favorite bands' CDs or tapes. Try to get an autographed picture or publicity shots of his favorite singer or band, or some unique Western artwork or jewelry. Place the tapes or CDs and country items in a Western or Mexican blanket, and hand it to him all bundled up.

EXAMPLE

My husband loves Patsy Kline, so for my country music gift I bought him the videotape of the movie about Patsy Kline's life, a cassette tape of her music, a book of her life, and postage stamps with her picture that had recently been issued by the US Post Office. I then typed the words from one of her songs, "Crazy," on paper, which I used to wrap the video tape. On the outside of the gift box I wrote "Crazy about You." When he opened the box and saw all of the Patsy Kline memorabilia, I could see how happy the entire gift had made him.

Gift Idea
42

COOKIE JAR

IS YOUR PARTNER a **cookie monster?** Bake him his favorite cookies and present them to him in a cookie jar just for him. If you are not sure what his favorite cookie is, call his mother and ask her what he liked the most as a child—she may even have the recipe for them.

Include a small note in the cookie jar telling him that you promise to refill the cookie jar every month for a year, or for however long you want to do it.

TIPS

See if his mother still has an old cookie jar from his childhood, and ask to borrow it as a special surprise.

Bake a huge cookie from the recipe he likes the most.

Gift Idea
43

COFFEE LOVER

IF YOUR PARTNER LOVES COFFEE and drinks it all day, everyday, buy him a small **espresso/cappuccino machine** and a coffee grinder with a bag of fresh roasted coffee beans. With this gift you can include a jumbo coffee cup or a travel mug for his car. With some non-lead based paint, write a personal message on the bottom of the mug. The message can be very personal, because only he will be able to read it and understand.

EXTRA
Add a fresh basket of homemade muffins or cookies with the coffee.

Gift Idea
44

THE BEACH BOY

WHEN YOU HAVE a partner who loves **sailing and the sea**, buy him gifts having to do with the water. You can frame posters of the sea, sailboats, or dolphins. Pick up a tape or CD of the sounds of the waves or a waterfall. A small aquarium with tropical fish makes a very exotic gift. Or for a special treat, give him all the presents together.

CHOICE
Another gift is a big beach towel in a beach bag with other beach accessories that he may need.

Gift Idea
45

NEW SPORTS JACKET

A UNIQUE WAY TO PRESENT a new sports jacket as a gift is to include a **surprise dinner** with it. Get a menu from his favorite restaurant and place it inside one of the jacket pockets. Write on the menu when he should meet you there. Put the jacket in a box and send it to him while he is at work. After work he will meet you at the restaurant, wearing the new jacket. All you have to bring is yourself.

TIPS

Bring along a shirt and a tie for him if the restaurant is formal.

You can use this idea for any type of coat—try a sleek leather jacket.

Gift Idea
46

NEW WALLET

WHEN IT IS TIME to buy him a new **wallet** and you want to add a nice surprise to it, take a picture of yourself, trim it to credit card size, and write a message on the back of the picture. Laminate the picture in order to make it look like one of his credit cards. Purchase the wallet that you like and put the picture inside the new wallet. For good luck, add a $10 dollar bill. These two additions to this gift symbolize your wishes for him—that his wallet will be always full of money and his heart will always be full of love for you.

Wrap this gift with wrapping paper designed to look like money and place a folded dollar bill through the knot of the bow.

TIPS

You can make the wrapping paper yourself by pasting some fake paper money onto a plain white sheet of paper.

Remember that the important part of this gift is your picture.

Gift Idea
47

HERSHEY'S KISSES

GIVE YOUR PARTNER a Hershey's Kiss to remember. Make a **paperweight** that will look like a BIG Hershey's Kiss. You can use plaster to make a cone shape for this gift, or use any cardboard or plastic material in the shape of a cone.

Wrap the cone shape with gold or silver paper to resemble a Kiss. Remember to place a white strip of paper hanging out of the top of the cone with your personal message on it, such as "I love you," or "Let's Kiss."

IDEA
Put your phone number on the strip of paper (so he will be reminded to call more often).

Gift Idea
48

MANICURE & PEDICURE

IF YOUR PARTNER IS CONSERVATIVE IN THINKING and believes manicures and pedicures are only for women, go ahead and surprise him—take him out and treat him to a **manicure and/or pedicure.** Sit him down in the chair and have two women work on him at once, one doing the pedicure and foot massage, and the other manicuring his nails. The fact that you are "forcing" him to have this done can be flattering for your man. Also, all of the personal attention he will get will make him feel wonderfully pampered.

EXPERIENCE

When I saw my husband sitting in the chair, it was apparent how much he enjoyed this gift (even though he did not want to admit it).

— CHAPTER FOUR —

Sports Fan

🐦 🐦 🐦

No matter how long you
and your partner have been together,
the little extra attention you give
to his hobby shows how much he
means to you. Whether his love is
golf, fishing, gambling, or just
watching sports on TV,
you can still find a gift to
fulfill his love for his sports hobby.

Gift Idea
49

ROAD TRIP!

IF YOUR PARTNER IS A BIG baseball, football, or basketball fan, but his favorite team is not a local one, plan a road trip so he can see them in action. Buy the tickets, book airline reservations or gas up the car, reserve a hotel room, and get packed. The night at the hotel can be a **weekend getaway** which can turn into a mini-honeymoon.

To present the gift, place all of the tickets and reservation information into a cap or T-shirt with his team's logo. He will be blown away, and you will have a little getaway for yourself. (It is even better if you are a sports fan, too!)

TIPS

This gift works well even if his team is local (you will save the transportation costs, too).

You need to prepare this gift ahead of time. Make sure he will be free that weekend.

Gift Idea
50

BIRTHDAY WITH FRIENDS

Plan a surprise birthday gift with a friend who shares the same **hobby** as your partner. You may choose to plan this gift with four couples. So when the men play golf together, the women may prefer to play tennis, swim, or get a massage.

After you find the right friends, look for the golf resort. Don't let the men know about the surprise, so they will all be surprised together.

Most packages include three meals a day, so prepare with the hotel manager in advance to help you with your surprise. You will need to arrange for a cake or special meal for his birthday.

TIP

If you would like to prepare this gift for only the two of you, most resorts have guests who will be looking for someone to fill their golf group. Look in golf magazines for resorts.

Gift Idea
51

THE GOLFER

FOR A PARTNER WHO IS CRAZY ABOUT GOLF, there are many items you can get for him at the Pro Shop that he can use. If you are not sure what to get for him, **golf balls** are always useful to every golfer. When you know what kind of golf balls he uses, buy them. To personalize them, buy a golf ball monogrammer and monogram them yourself with his initials. It may take a lot of time, but in the end it will be worth the trouble. He will always be able to tell which golf balls are his when golfing with others.

TIPS

The significance of this gift is he does not have to monogram the golf balls himself.

Buy him golf balls for each year of his age.

Place the golf balls back into the original box.

Gift Idea

52

RETIREMENT GIFT II

IF IN A FEW YEARS you and your husband are planning to retire and he shows an interest in golf, buy him a set of **beginner golf clubs.** (Ask a golf pro which clubs are best for beginners.) Along with the clubs, buy a series of golf lessons—for the two of you!

This is a very original gift which *both* of you can share and enjoy during your retirement years.

OPTIONS

This idea works for any sports activity he likes.

You can use this new sports interest for ideas for later gifts (new clubs, golf attire, greens' fees).

Sports Fan

Gift Idea

53

"BUSINESS" TOWEL

SURPRISE HIM WITH A "BUSINESS" TOWEL. This towel can be any size, but a golf towel will probably work best for this idea. Take your partner's **business card** and have it duplicated on the towel. This can be done through a store that embroiders names on uniforms, or use your own sewing machine or fabric paint from a craft store. It is not hard to do and usually only needs one color of paint.

EXAMPLE

My husband's business card reads, "Have Clubs, Will Play," along with his name and telephone number. I made him a golf towel with the same information. Now, everyone knows which golf bag is his.

Even if your partner does not have a business card, you can still make the towel look like a business card with his name, address, and phone number on it.

Gift Idea
54

GIFT CERTIFICATE

WHEN YOU FIND THAT YOU ARE STILL PUZZLED over what to buy your partner after you have exhausted all possibilities of finding that special gift, buy him a **gift certificate.** This gift still requires some intuition and knowledge of what your man would like.

If he has a favorite hobby, look for a hobby store. If he has a favorite sport, find the biggest sport store in your neighborhood. Look for a place where the selection will be large. He will feel like a kid in a toy store.

When you are on a budget or you want him to be able to choose among the big ticket items, then ask his family and friends to participate in this gift.

Place the gift certificate into a large gift box.

TIP

Make sure that the gift certificate does not have an expiration date, so he can use this gift at any time and for everything, such as his hobby supplies— golf balls, fishing tackle, or tools.

Gift Idea

55

EXERCISE ROOM

TURN THAT SPARE ROOM in your home into a useful personal gift for him. Clean the room and buy him an exercise machine to place in it. If your already have some exercise equipment, transfer it to this "new" room. Add a small TV, some towels, a portable radio, and make the room into his **private gym.**

On his birthday, hand him the key to that room in a gift box.

OPTION
When you don't have a spare room yet have some yard space, buy a small storeroom or shed and make it into an exercise room.

Gift Idea

56

THE INVESTOR

"HAPPY BIRTHDAY!
YOU NOW OWN 100 SHARES OF
(insert company) CORPORATION"

THE STOCK MARKET can be a wonderful new hobby for your partner. Get him started by buying some **shares of stock** for him through a licensed broker or bank investor. Be sure to research stocks you are interested in before buying any shares.

Along with the stock certificate, buy him a three-month subscription to *Investor's Business Daily* or the *Wall Street Journal,* two daily newspapers that give valuable information on business and the stock market. Who knows, maybe this new hobby will make you millionaires!

TIP

Include a magnifying glass with this gift (when you see the stock market list, you will understand why).

Gift Idea
57

HIS SPORT HERO

DOES YOUR PARTNER HAVE A SPORTS HERO from his childhood? Today, there are many baseball and football memorabilia stores where you can find a **one-of-a-kind item** that he will treasure.

Ask his childhood friends, his brothers and sisters, or his parents who his sports hero was during his childhood. Visit one of these stores and ask to see what they have with this sport hero's name or signature on it.

For added enjoyment, give him an additional gift such as a baseball glove with his name on it, or a baseball card with his hero's name.

This gift can become something very meaningful, that he can pass on to his children.

TIP
Some of these stores are linked through a network of dealers throughout the country to help you find just what you are looking for.

Gift Idea

58

MINI TELEVISION

IS YOUR PARTNER A SPORTS FANATIC, one of those men who watches sports on TV all weekend long and doesn't want to leave the house? Buy him a **mini portable TV.** You can buy him any one of a variety of sizes and styles—there is even one that will fit in his pocket or he can use in his car. This way he can leave the house and pursue other activities without missing his sports events.

But, if you know that he will *never* leave the house when his sport shows are on TV, buy the 13" TV. You know that in the long run, you will be the one using the mini-TV, while he is watching the bigger screen.

TIPS

Buy him a T-shirt that says something funny like "King of the Remote Control."

Even if you will be the one who ends up with the mini-TV, you will have still given him a gift personalized for him.

Sports Fan **65**

― CHAPTER FIVE ―

Cakes, Dinners, and Flowers

❧ ❧ ❧

When you stop giving each other gifts, but you still want to surprise your partner, here are some plain, yet unique ideas for flowers, dinner invitations, and plain birthday cakes—as well as how to make them different with the little extras you put into them. This can melt his heart and bring tears to his eyes.

Gift Idea 59

A PIECE OF CAKE

IF YOU DO NOT WANT TO MAKE A BIG DEAL about his birthday but still want him to know you remembered it, buy a big **ice cream cake** and have it decorated especially for him. Buy plastic spoons, napkins, and plates. If the napkins are not already decorated, decorate them yourself by writing "Happy Birthday" with a colored pen or marker. Wrap everything in a large box and have it delivered to his office for a little party for him with his co-workers. Maybe it's only a birthday cake, but it does show your love.

TIPS

Pick a funny decoration or words for the cake.

Instead of a cake, have a pizza delivered with "Happy Birthday" spelled out in toppings.

Gift Idea
60

NO BIG DEAL!
BIRTHDAY CAKE

IF YOUR PARTNER IS THE TYPE WHO SAYS, "No parties and no gifts," then you can either make him a **small cake** yourself, or buy a cake decorated with whatever saying or design you want on it. The cake is not really the point of this gift; the main idea here is to order special napkins with your man's name and the date of the event on them.

These napkins can be ordered and purchased at stationery stores or print shops. It is not expensive to have these printed, but it does take two or three weeks for the napkins to be personalized.

TIPS

You can have the bakery make the cake in the shape of a heart or decorated with items from his favorite sport.

You can have personal messages printed on the napkins, too. And of course, don't forget to invite your family to the "cake party."

Cakes, Dinners, and Flowers

Gift Idea
61

THE BOX IN THE BIRTHDAY CAKE

A BIRTHDAY CAKE AS A GIFT BOX can be an idea for a surprise party. Bake a big birthday cake and leave or make a large **hole** in the middle of the cake. After the cake is ready, place a cardboard box inside the cake to hide your gift. Then, cover the cake with icing and your favorite decorations.

He will find his surprise when he cuts the cake in front of all his guests.

If you bake a square cake, you can use a larger box. He will never guess what is hidden in the cake.

TIPS

Don't forget to hide the cake. He may see it and be tempted to taste it.

This idea is good for smaller gifts like "Coin from His Birth Year," or "Car Keychain" (without the massage chair, of course)

Make a mark on the cake where the box is located so you can instruct him where to begin slicing.

70 *Show Him Your Love*

Gift Idea
62

FORTUNE COOKIES

THIS GIFT IS A FUN WAY TO SURPRISE HIM with your private message. Buy fortune cookies and cut them in half, or look for open cracks and try to pull out the "factory" messages. Replace them with your own private, intimate, **personal messages.** If you like, you can alter the existing message with your own humor or with small red hearts.

When you cut the cookies in half and want to stick them back together, melt some chocolate in a small saucepan (use low heat and stir constantly). Use a small pastry brush and "glue" the cookies back together with chocolate.

After the cookies have been "glued" back together, dip the wide end of the cookie in the melted chocolate to cover the repair you made. Place the finished cookies on waxed paper to dry.

TIPS

If you live in a big city, you can call the companies that make fortune cookies and order cookies with your own messages.

Be creative with your messages.

Try to surprise him. ——— *You can also roll the cookie dipped in chocolate with chopped almonds.*

Cakes, Dinners, and Flowers

Gift Idea
63

LUNCH FOR HIS BIRTHDAY

ON HIS BIRTHDAY, when he thinks that you have forgotten all about him, send a **special lunch** to his office. Make it his favorite food, which can be from a special restaurant or something you make in your own kitchen.

To make it into a party, send his entire office lunch at the same time and add a bottle of champagne (if his boss does not mind).

TIP
Send invitations to this lunch to everyone in his office and make it a birthday lunch party.

Gift Idea
64

TRANSPORT TO JAPAN

AS HE WALKS THROUGH THE FRONT DOOR, send him straight into the bathroom to have a bath. Make sure you have a tub full of hot water waiting for him. Shampoo his head and shave him, being sure to have plenty of hot towels on hand.

While he is getting dressed, continue with the preparation of the evening. Have a Japanese beer or hot *sake* ready for him. Serve sushi and other Japanese dishes on a small table in the middle of the room, using throw pillows for him to sit on, unless you have a futon that provides more seating area.

After you have both enjoyed this meal, give him a body massage. Don't be insulted if he falls asleep during the massage, take it as a compliment—it means he is enjoying the relaxing evening very much.

TIPS

Rent a kimono *to wear.* —— *Play Japanese music while you serve the dinner.*

Gift Idea 65

DINNER VIA TELEGRAM

ANOTHER DINNER INVITATION IDEA is to send your partner a telegram delivered by a person in a costume or a sports hero look-alike. If he likes blondes, have a **"blonde bombshell"** deliver the telegram inviting him to dinner at your home.

When he arrives for dinner, be waiting for him with a professional waiter to serve him his favorite meal from his favorite restaurant. You should not only surprise him with this special invitation, but with other gifts waiting at home.

TIPS

Make sure to send this telegram to his place of work.

After dinner, you will be free from having to do the dishes and can spend time with your partner in other ways.

Gift Idea
66

LIMO RIDE TO DINNER

TO MAKE HIS BIRTHDAY DINNER SPECIAL, rent a **limousine** to drive him to and from a restaurant. You can either arrange to have the limousine pick you both up together, or have it pick you up first so you can greet him when he opens the car door. What a surprise when he sees the limousine pull up with you in it!

If your dinner is at home, roll out a red rug in front of your door so he will have a royal entrance.

TIPS

Have flowers and champagne waiting in the limousine.

You can have friends waiting at the restaurant as a surprise for him.

Send a taxi to pick him up if you cannot find a limo service.

Cakes, Dinners, and Flowers

Gift Idea
67

SURPRISE ON THE BUS

A UNIQUE WAY TO SURPRISE your partner would be to **rent a bus** with a driver for the evening. So what if it is going to be expensive. This is a once-in-a-lifetime gift!

Have the driver pick up you and your partner first, then continue to pick up the other guests who are waiting at a designated spot or at their houses. The idea of this gift is that by the time you get to the restaurant, you will have all the guests with you.

After the first couple gets on the bus, your partner will think that he knows the surprise, but the surprise will continue as long as he remains curious about who else will be getting on the bus at the next stop. You can choose an out-of-town restaurant that has dinner and dancing, so that everyone will have a enjoyable evening together.

TIPS

You can pick up your partner as the last person on the bus.

Serve wine and/or champagne on the bus.

Inscribe the wine bottle with the day of the event.

Show Him Your Love

Gift Idea
68

YOURSELF AS A GIFT

PUT A BIG BOW AROUND YOURSELF, attach some balloons, and try to make yourself look like a gift. Attach a card that says "I am your gift for your birthday."

To avoid unexpected requests from him about what it is that he wants you to do, the card should contain a list from which he can choose. The ideas can be romantic, practical, or just plain fun. Let him mark off what he would like for his birthday.

Examples:
- ☐ Wash my car
- ☐ Make me a home-cooked meal
- ☐ Give me a full-body massage
- ☐ Have my favorite dinners ready for me one week
- ☐ Leave…me…alone!

TIPS

Make your list to suit your own preferences.

You can leave one line empty on the list for him to fill in.

Gift Idea
69

BIRTHDAY FLOWERS

IF YOU DECIDE TO CELEBRATE HIS BIRTHDAY with only flowers, **GO FOR IT.** Give your partner flowers all day long. Put flowers in places he would not expect: in the medicine cabinet, in the shower, inside the newspaper, in the refrigerator, on his car seat, in his briefcase, and his lunch bag. Have flowers sent to him while he is at work, and greet him with a bouquet upon his arrival home.

OPTION: *Tape little romantic notes on some of the flower stems.*

Gift Idea
70

ROSES TO
MAKE HIM BLUSH!

MOST MEN GIVE RED ROSES TO THEIR WOMEN. I have rarely heard of women giving roses to their men. Why not surprise him with a **box of red roses?** Send the roses to him while he is at work. He may blush on the outside, but he will be happy and proud on the inside. Put a birthday card inside the box thanking him for coming into your life. He will be flattered!

OPTIONS

Send him the same number of roses as his age.

To help him remember this gift, buy a vase and write a message to him on it.

Gift Idea
71

ROSES 4 HIM

ANOTHER UNIQUE WAY TO GIVE YOUR PARTNER FLOWERS is to pick **four colors of roses,** such as yellow, white, pink, and red, Each color will symbolize a different meaning. Next, attach four cards to one rose of each color explaining its meaning: "This yellow rose stands for the good friendship we have in our partnership;" "From the beginning, our love was as pure as this white rose;" "To this day our love is as sweet and full of happiness as this pink rose;" and "After all of our years together, we still have the love and passion of this red rose."

You can follow this chart to choose which colors you want to give your partner.

TIPS
Look for cards that express these special meanings:
love, friendship, and purity.

ROSES
DIFFERENT COLORS, DIFFERENT MEANINGS

Color	Symbolism
red	love, passion
light pink	grace, joy
dark pink	thankfulness
white	innocence, purity
yellow	friendship, respect
coral	desire
lavender	enchantment
orange	fascination
black	mystery
red & white	unity

Cakes, Dinners, and Flowers

— CHAPTER SIX —

Paintings, Pictures, and Calendars

🌱🌱🌱

Love can be shown in many different ways. One
way is to choose and buy a present for the one
you love. Another way is to go beyond the normal
expectations of a gift by creating it yourself.
Either way, he will love the gifts on all of these pages,
and will know you are the one responsible for the
gifts that hang on his wall or lay on his desk.
Can you imagine how moved he will be to learn
that you created them yourself?

Gift Idea
72

EMOTIONAL GIFT

AN EMOTIONAL AND SENSITIVE GIFT for your partner may be a **portrait of a loved one** who has passed away, perhaps a parent or a grandparent. Find a picture of this person when he or she was young. Give the photo to an artist to create a charcoal portrait. Make sure the photo you give the artist is large and clear enough to assure an accurate reproduction.

The sensitive nature of this gift requires a special wrapping style. Don't wrap it in just any paper. Wrap it in something that will make him laugh at first to take away from the emotionalism of the gift.

Painters usually charge about $50 for a charcoal sketch of one person. A good place to find a talented artist is at any art fair or in an art school. Look at the artist's portfolio to be sure his or her style is compatible with the way you want the portrait drawn.

TIPS

If you live in an area where it may be difficult to find an artist, have the photograph enlarged to poster size and then frame it. Use a black and white photograph.

For my partner, I wrapped the picture in humorously decorated underwear.

Gift Idea
73

PAINTED PICTURE

FIND A PICTURE OF YOUR PARTNER you really like and take it to a professional artist to paint. Tell the artist to paint a scene with your partner doing his **favorite activity**. If he enjoys fishing, have the artist paint him fishing in a boat or on the shores of a beautiful stream or lake. If he enjoys golfing, let the main background of the picture be a golf course. The painter will paint the background that you prefer.

Artists can be expensive, but you can always try a local art school, or in special places like hotels or at street fairs. The painting doesn't have to be a really fine piece of art. What makes this gift special is that you didn't just have a simple portrait painted. You put extra thought into this gift by choosing a background that is special to him.

EXAMPLE

I gave an artist a picture of my husband, sitting on the grass. He painted a picture of my husband with a golf course as the background.

Gift Idea 74

YOUR HEART'S ON CANVAS

THIS NEXT GIFT IS AN ORIGINAL IDEA you can make yourself. Buy a canvas stretched on a wood frame, any size that you prefer. Get several colors of acrylic paint and **paint lots of hearts,** as many as you want, all over the board.

You can leave the background white or paint it any color you desire.

In addition to the hearts, paint the words "My heart's full of love for you," or "I love you with all my hearts!" or "With lots of love."

You can also paint one large heart on the canvas made up from many little hearts. Write your message inside the large heart.

TIPS

This is a wonderful Valentine's Day gift.

This is also a great gift for no reason at all.

86 *Show Him Your Love*

Gift Idea
75

ACTION PICTURES

DO YOU WATCH YOUR PARTNER while he engages in his favorite sport or activity, like fishing, basketball, baseball, or tennis? Buy some high-speed film and **take a photo of him** while he is performing this activity. Shoot many pictures so you will have lots of action shots to choose from. Take the pictures you like and have them framed. Frame from six to twelve photos, putting each picture in sequence. The finished product should look like frozen frames from a movie. Professional framers can do a wonderful job putting these photos together for you.

REMEMBER
When you take the pictures, make sure he does not realize what you are doing. You want this to be a surprise.

Gift Idea
76

SIGNED FAMILY PHOTO

AN EXCELLENT GIFT is to have a **family portrait** taken at a photo studio. Have the picture enlarged. Black and white photos work the best for this gift.

Prior to framing the portrait, have everyone in the photo write something personal on it. For example, a child may write, "Dad, I love you," or "Dad, remember when...." If there are more than a few people in the photo, have each person autograph the picture near his or her picture.

TIP
This is an ideal Father's Day Gift.

Gift Idea
77

FRAMED ITEM

THERE ARE SPECIALTY STORES that sell large framed photos of famous rock stars, actors, and sports figures. These framed pictures not only include the photo of the famous person, but also have words written on them by that person. These pictures can sell for as much as $200 to $500.

Make a similar photo of your partner. Find an old photo of your partner along with other **memorabilia,** such as an old love letter that he sent to you, his high school diploma, or other things that would be important to him. Frame these pieces together and you will have a collection for him.

TIPS

Visit the specialty stores that sell these photos to get different ideas of how to put together this gift.

His mother may be a good source of items for this gift.

Gift Idea
78

FRAMED CARTOON

A GLASS-FRAMED CARTOON can make a fun gift. To add even more to this already fun gift, write a personal note or just a simple "I Love You" on the glass with a black marker.

When I gave this gift to my husband, I bought a funny picture of two cartoon characters playing golf. I then wrote on the glass:

Lubi Lubi Lubi Lu
How Much I Love You I Wish I Knew
Happy Birthday To You

I also applied heavy lipstick to my lips and kissed all over the glass, covering the entire picture.

TIP
This also makes a great Valentine's Day gift, or a gift for no reason at all.

Gift Idea
79

YOUR SONG

WHEN YOU HAVE A SONG THAT YOU BOTH LIKE, or if his favorite song is a **love song,** make him a surprise by putting the words from that song onto a large white poster board. Put yellow highlighter on the words and sentences that express your feelings for him. Have this surprise framed and wrapped. When you present it to him, have the song playing in the background.

If you don't have a song that belongs to the two of you, you can always make this gift with a song you like. This makes a wonderful gift to hang in his office.

TIPS

This gift is a good idea as a birthday card.

Music stores are your best bet for finding sheet music.

Gift Idea
80

A BIRTHDAY CARD TO REMEMBER

TAKE A SMALL PIECE of cardboard or poster board and have all his friends, family, and co-workers write a personal message on it. Encourage everyone to write **special words or messages** for him. Frame the finished project as if it were an expensive piece of artwork and present it to him at his party.

You can do something similar by using a picture of your partner and gluing it to the poster board and then have all his friends sign their names around the picture.

TIPS

This gift can be combined with the "Surprise on the Bus" on page 76.

Use a picture from his childhood.

Gift Idea
81

HIS PRIVATE CALENDAR

CREATE A PRIVATE CALENDAR for your partner that is **for his eyes only.** Go to a professional photographer who specializes in portraits (you may feel more comfortable with a woman). Have the photographer take twelve photographs of you in the following manner:

- For January, take a picture of you fully dressed in winter clothing
- For February, take a piece of clothing off
- For March, take another piece off
- Continue on for each month until…(get the point!)
- For the December photo, you can choose to wear a swimsuit, a towel, or…it's up to you.

TIP

If you would like the calendar to be more sexy, start with a very skimpy outfit that has twelve parts to it. For example, dress in a bathing suit, lingerie, and stockings with a garter, hat, and jewelry.

Gift Idea
82

ONE-MONTH CALENDAR

FOR THE MONTH OF YOUR PARTNER'S BIRTHDAY, make a **special calendar.** Take a large piece of blank paper and on the bottom half draw or paste the calendar for his birthday month, circling the date of his birthday.

The top half of the calendar is reserved for you to place something special, like the words of a love song or a picture. Frame this single page one-month calendar and hang it on his wall.

DECEMBER 1995
Best wishes on your special day
I love you with all my heart

		1	2	3	4	♡5
6	7	8	9	10	11	12
13	14	15	16	17	18	19
20	21	22	23	24	25	26
27	28	29	30	31		

TIPS

This gift can be used when you give him more than one gift.

Write the year on this calendar, so he can remember the birthday this particular gift was given to him.

Gift Idea
83

APPOINTMENT CALENDAR

EVEN IF HE REALLY DOES NOT NEED ONE, buy him an appointment calendar or organizer. Fill in this calendar with all the dates of his **family's and friends' birthdays and anniversaries.** Fill in any other special dates you would like him to remember. You can write in phone numbers and addresses next to the entry for each person. If he does not have time or does not like to shop for cards, include pre-purchased cards with stamped envelopes as part of the gift.

TIPS

Draw small hearts next to the special events for both of you on the calendar.

He will not forget your birthday after you have given him this gift.

— CHAPTER SEVEN —

More than One Gift

❧ ❧ ❧

After many years of being together, sometimes you run out of ideas of what to buy for your partner. You still want to surprise him and show him you care, but how? More than one gift can refresh your relationship and bring fun, humor, and romance back into your lives. Make the number of gifts meaningful, like his age, the number of months or years you have been together, or how many days until your wedding.

Gift Idea 84

MORE THAN ONE GIFT, HOW

WHEN YOU DECIDE to give your partner **several gifts at once,** but you don't know where to begin, here are some suggestions.

Go through your partner's personal effects and look for things that he needs like a new toothbrush, razor, hair dryer, pajamas, or slippers, and take notes. All the gifts can be related to a single theme or subject, such as an outfit for work (shirt, tie, cuff links, tie clips, socks, and shoes) wrapped individually with notes and messages on each one, or wrapped all together.

You can fill his car, office, or home with small gifts. Put them in places he will be sure to find them. Be sure to tell him how many gifts there are, so he will know when to stop looking!

TIP

A holiday sale is a great time to purchase most of his gifts. You can buy them and hide them until it is the perfect time to give them.

Gift Idea
85

MORE THAN ONE GIFT, WHEN

IF YOU LIKE THE IDEA OF GIVING MULTIPLE GIFTS, an excellent way to find gifts that can be the basis for ideas in this chapter is to go to a party store that sells **humorous gifts.** A few ways to make the gifts meaningful are:

1. If he is going to be 45 years old (or whatever age he is approaching), then give him his first gift 45 days before his birthday and continue to give him a gift every day for the next 45 days.

2. Make an entire birthday month for him by giving him 30 days of funny gift giving, one gift per day. Start the presentations 15 days before his birthday and continue on for 15 days after his birthday.

TIPS

Souvenir stores have funny gifts to offer, too.

Prepare well ahead of time for this gift giving.

Gift Idea 86

A GIFT EACH HOUR

A FUN WAY TO MAKE your partner's special day last **from morning till night** is to give him one gift every hour. Buy him twelve gifts and instruct him that he can only open one each hour.

Label each gift with a time to be opened: "Open at 9:00 AM" or "Open at 3:00 PM," so that if he has to work that day, he will have specific instructions as to when he should open each gift. If his job does not permit him to open a gift each hour, you can modify your opening instructions to fit within his break schedules.

Some ideas for gifts can include a coffee mug for the first present. The lunchtime gift can be an invitation to meet you for lunch. Guide him to a restaurant or wait outside with a picnic for a romantic midday rendezvous.

At dinner time, you can give him a romantic card with a map or a puzzle indicating a restaurant for him to meet you at. The dinner can be a gift, or you can prepare his favorite meal at home. Of course, these gifts do not have to end with dinner. Use your imagination.

TIPS

You can write out his gift-opening schedule on a piece of paper or write it in his day planner.

You can create personal gift certificates for presents you made, which he can redeem later on in the day.

Gift Idea
87

SEVEN-DAY GIFT

LET YOUR PARTNER KNOW that you intend to give him **seven gifts** starting six days before his birthday. Each day you will give him a new gift.

On the first, second, third, fourth, and fifth days, give him small gifts that show your love (you can get small gift ideas from other chapters and at the end of this book). On day six, the last day of his current birthday, throw him a surprise party. He will not be expecting a party before his birthday! (The party is his gift for the day.)

On day seven, his birthday, surprise him with another party. Yes! Another party. He will never expect you to throw a party one day after another! This time the party is to celebrate his turning a new age.

You can choose whether to go all out with these parties, keep them small, or make one big and one small. Buy balloons and streamers to really decorate your house. You can invite half of his friends for one party, and the other half for the second one, or invite them all to both. Let the guests know that they do not have to bring two gifts. The real intent here is to celebrate and have two parties.

Your partner will love you for not only remembering his birthday, but for also celebrating the age he is leaving behind. This is truly a once-in-a-lifetime gift.

OPTIONS

One of the parties can be a pizza party (saving you time in the kitchen).

Order party hats and T-shirts with his name on it for party revelers to wear.

Order two birthday cakes, one for the last day of his previous age and one for the first day of his new age.

Gift Idea
88

THE TWELVE DAYS OF CHRISTMAS

USE THE TRADITION of the **twelve days** of Christmas as a sample to celebrate your man's birthday. For example:
- For the first day, give him a gift of your choice.
- For the second day, send two slippers.
- For the third day, hand him three certificates to wash his car.
- For the fourth day, send him four aftershave lotions (for home, office, car, and a spare).
- For the fifth day, give him five greeting cards.
- For the sixth day, send him six T-shirts.
- For the seventh day, present him with his seven favorite snacks or desserts.
- For the eighth day, give him eight pairs of underwear.
- For the ninth day, surprise him with nine roses.
- For the tenth day, give him ten ties.
- For the eleventh day, send him eleven balloons.
- For the twelfth day, buy him twelve pairs of socks (or six pair to make up twelve single socks).

TIPS

For each day's gift, send or place the present in unusual places—his office, fitness center, mother's house, his house, or when he visits his barber.

You can choose to celebrate his birthday for the next eleven months and create a "countdown" calendar to mark the remaining months until his birthday.

Gift Idea

89

A GIFT FOR EACH YEAR

BUY YOUR MAN A GIFT for each **year of his life.** (If your man is 50 years old or more, this could get expensive. An option is to put years together in groups of three, four, or five. Give him a gift for each group of years.) You can present all these gifts any way you want. Following are two ideas.

One way to present all these gifts is to place them all in a wheelbarrow and roll the wheelbarrow in the middle of the living room. Write on each gift what year (or years) it is for.

Another way to present these gifts is to spread them all over your house or apartment so he can find a gift in every corner. For example, when he gets up in the morning, you can have a new toothbrush, underwear, and towel ready for him. When he goes to the kitchen, he can find a new coffee mug. Put a note in it that says, "More to Come."

OPTION *You can make the gifts symbolize other anniversaries important in your man's life, like the days, months, or years you have been together. For example, I gave my husband gifts for the eight wonderful months we were together, and labeled each one with a month (March, July, etc.).*

Gift Idea
90

SHABBY BAG

MY PARTNER HAD A HANDBAG THAT HE LOVED and carried with him on every vacation we took. He used this bag for all of his personal effects, medicines, and books.

Because the bag was made of fabric, it wore out quickly and looked shabby with age. Since I was unable to replace this old bag with a similar one, I found a tailor who was able to **make a new one** exactly like the old bag. I choose however to make the new bag out of leather so it would wear better. When I presented the bag to my partner for our first year anniversary, I put 12 small gifts inside the new bag to represent the 12 months that we had been married. Each gift was wrapped separately with the name of the month on the outside. From the look on his face, I could tell that he had never received a gift like this before.

TIP
Ask the tailor to put your special message in gold lettering inside the bag.

Gift Idea
91

BIRTHSTONES

A unique gift idea that can contain his birthstone is a **money clip** made from gold. After purchasing the clip, buy a special gemstone that symbolizes his birthday. Ask your jeweler to mount the stone on the money clip you have chosen. In addition, ask the jeweler to engrave your special message on the back of the money clip.

If he doesn't need a new money clip, but he loves jewelry, surprise him with a date calendar charm with his birthstone mounted on the actual date of his birth.

TIP
The date calendar charm can be attached to his key chain.

MONTH	BIRTHSTONE	COLOR
January	Garnet	Dark Red
February	Amethyst	Dark Violet
March	Aquamarine	Light Blue
April	Diamond	Clear White
May	Emerald	Green
June	Pearl *or* Alexandrite	White, Pink, Black Khaki
July	Ruby	Red
August	Peridot	Pale Green
September	Sapphire	Blue
October	Opal	Multi-color on White
November	Topaz	Yellow/Blue
December	Turquoise *or* Blue Zircon	Turquoise Blue

— Chapter Eight —

When Money Is Not a Problem

🍂 🍂 🍂

The following gift ideas are relatively expensive compared to the previous chapters, and they will take some time to prepare. But they are also unforgettable and worth every penny. These gifts are for you too—most of them are gifts that are shared. Which are, of course, the best kind. He will never forget any of these gifts, and deep in your heart you will know that this time, you did it right.

Gift Idea
92

TALK RADIO FAN

IF YOU PARTNER IS A BIG FAN of a **radio celebrity**, and you want to somehow incorporate it into a gift idea, do what I did! My partner is an incredible loyal Rush Limbaugh fan. He admires Limbaugh so much he would set the alarm clock every night for his television show and have me record the radio show every morning for him to listen to later. I thought I should give him a gift having to do with Rush Limbaugh.

Several months before my partner's birthday, I made plane reservations to New York, set up hotel accommodations, and got tickets to the Rush Limbaugh television show. For four months, I kept my plans a secret.

Two hours before we were to leave, he found out about the tickets. (Don't let this happen to you.) I think he saw them in my purse. Anyway, it was still a surprise even then. We went to New York and saw the show three nights in a row, and got a video of the shows. I don't think this will be the last time my partner sees Limbaugh, but it sure will be a time he will never forget!

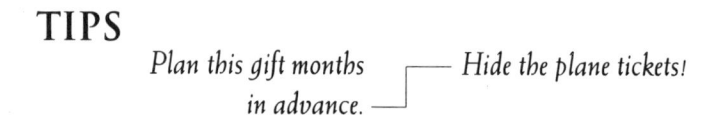

TIPS

Plan this gift months in advance.

Hide the plane tickets!

Gift Idea
93

COUNTRY
MUSIC VACATION

IF YOUR PARTNER REALLY LOVED the "Country Music Fan" gift idea, he will absolutely flip when you present him with tickets to **Nashville, Tennessee.** Your travel agent can set you up with an inclusive package for airlines, hotel, and shows. Try to arrange to see as many shows as possible while you are there.

To make the gift even more special, add a cowboy hat, bolo tie, and cowboy boots. Put everything in a large western basket or blanket. You may either take this package along with you on the trip, or arrange to have it waiting at the hotel. All these accessories will make the trip more special when attending the shows or touring this country music town, and wearing the proper attire.

TIPS

This gift requires planning ahead of time.

A weekend trip can be an option.

Gift Idea
94

FISHING WEEKEND

IF YOUR PARTNER LOVES TO FISH, then surprise him by renting a **motor home for a weekend.** Yes, a motor home. Take him out for an "Eat, Sleep, and Fish" vacation.

Hide your secret by asking him to join you for a weekend getaway. Rent and hide all the necessary fishing gear in the motor home the day you will pick him up. Put a large sign on it saying "My Best Catch of the Day," or hand him a card with a fish hook on it saying "Hooked on You."

Your partner is sure to be floored when you pull up in that motor home.

OPTION: *Have T-shirts and baseball hats made with "Eat, Sleep, & Fish" printed on them*

Gift Idea
95

FORCED VACATION

FOR THIS NEXT GIFT YOU WILL NEED a lot of courage and, above all, a relationship with you partner's boss, secretary, or any other of his associates to help you with this surprise.

Ask his boss, or maybe his associates, to send him on a **"phony" business trip** during his birthday. The trip can be to another city or even another country.

Once the business trip has been scheduled, you have several options:
- you can ask him if he would like you to join him on the trip since you would like to be with him on his birthday,
- you can get a ticket to be in the seat next to him on the plane, or
- you can surprise him in the hotel room.

Of course, you will want to immediately let him know that the entire trip was your plan for his birthday.

TIPS

Make this surprise fall on a Thursday or Friday so that you can spend the entire weekend together.

If you choose to surprise him on the flight, volunteer to drive him to the airport.

Gift Idea

96

FATHER AND CHILD

WHAT COULD BE A MORE THOUGHTFUL GIFT than to give your partner an unforgettable **vacation with his son or daughter?** This special gift could be a week camping and fishing in Alaska. A travel agency will be able to help you pick the perfect vacation along with arranging for transportation and lodging. This is a once-in-a-lifetime experience that will reinforce his relationship with his child.

TIPS

Make sure you plan this gift for the summer. Even if your partner's birthday is in winter, you can give this gift as something to look forward to.

Provide them with warm clothes and long underwear.

Gift Idea
97

SURPRISE ON A CRUISE

A SURPRISE PARTY ON A CRUISE is more fun when **celebrated with family and friends**. Make arrangements with his family and friends for them to be on the same cruise. Don't let your partner know that they are on the ship. Have them board before you, or maybe board in a different port. Let the crew know about the secret so they can help you set up the party. Watch the surprise on his face when he sees this party for him.

TIPS

This gift takes a lot of work and planning. Start at least one year before his birthday.

Have his family and friends bring birthday decorations.

Gift Idea
98

MASSAGE CHAIR

THIS GIFT IS GUARANTEED to add some **spice to your life.** Even though it may take you a year to save money for this gift, buy him an expensive massage chair for relaxing his back and neck. This chair has a special built-in computer for different shiatsu massages. It is made of leather and really looks worth the price you will pay. It may seem rather expensive, but wait until you see the expression on his face when he sits and relaxes in this wonderful chair.

TIPS

Place the chair in your bedroom.

Make sure to insure the chair.

I purchased this chair from a showroom so I paid only half of the original cost. My husband uses this chair at least once a day.

Gift Idea
99

SOMEONE LOVES YOU

YOU ARE ON A BUSINESS TRIP and are stuck in another city on your partner's birthday. Show him how much you love him from a **distance!** Send him a T-shirt that says "Someone in (city name) Loves You." Along with the shirt send flight tickets so he can meet you at your hotel.

If you do not want to spend the money for airline tickets, but still like the idea of this type of surprise, send a T-shirt with the words, "Someone in (name of hotel) Loves You." Rent a room at the hotel and send your partner the shirt with your hotel room number. At the hotel, wait for him with champagne on ice.

OPTION
Buy a silk robe or fancy boxer shorts for him to wear while he is there. Have them monogrammed with the date of this gift. Use your imagination.

When Money Is Not a Problem

Gift Idea
100

MUSICAL PARTNER

HAS YOUR PARTNER shown signs of **musical talent** or does he dream of playing an instrument? If so, surprise him with his favorite musical instrument and with a book on how to play that instrument.

If he already owns a musical instrument, a nice gift would be a neon sculpture of his instrument. The sculpture can also be any musical symbol such as notes, keyboards, and clefs. Wrap the gift with the sheet music of "your song."

TIPS

A pawn shop can be the right place to look for the instrument.

Don't forget a special "note" from you.

Gift Idea
101

CAR ON HIS BIRTHDAY

WHAT COULD BE MORE EXCITING for your partner than getting him **the car he has dreamed of?** *This does not mean that you should buy him a car!* Look in the rental car section for a sports car, a luxury car, or a special model that you know he would love to have. Rent the car for the weekend as a birthday gift.

After you have returned the car and gone back to your normal routine, surprise him again with a model car exactly like the car you rented. This will help him remember the special gift you gave him.

TIP
See if you can find the same car as the first car he owned.

― Chapter Nine ―

For Lovers *and* Others

🌹🌹🌹

Here are hundreds more gift ideas for men who love "toys," for office and car gifts, for sports fans, for gifts "just because," and, of course, for lovers and others.

FOR MEN WHO LOVE "TOYS"

Answering machine
Automatic card shuffle
Beer machine *(to brew beer)*
Binoculars
CD cleaner
Cellular phone holder
Compact disk storage
Crossword companion
Electric drill
Electric razor
Electric toothbrush
Electronic chess
   (with teaching program)
Game set *(any kind)*
Gold slinky
Grip strengthener
Hair dryer
Handyman's tool set
His personalized poker chips
Kite
Lighted electric tie rack
Lounger massage cushion

Lunch box
Magic tricks kit
Magnetic parts holder for the handyman
Mini travel alarm clock
Money belt
Panoramic camera
Personal book light
Personal groomer
Pocket knife
Portable steamer
Shower clock
Soundscape environment
Stock market tie
Tape measure key chain
Telescope
Therapeutic Chinese
   exercise balls
Toy for his special collection
Unique alarm clock
Video game
Walkman

OFFICE "TOYS"

365-day calendar with jokes
Air cleaner
Aquarium *(small)*
Ashtray that reduces smoke
Beverage warmer
Book stand
Brass bookmark *(engraved)*
Business card holder
Calligraphy set
Combination office organizer/luggage
Computer carrying case
Desk accessories
Desk globe of the world
Desk pad *(with family photo)*
Disk of solitaire games
Diskette holder
Electronic notebook
Envelope opener
Envelope sealer
Executive chair
Fax/copy machine *(portable)*
Glass nameplate
Headset for hands-free communication

Kaleidoscope
Laser pointer pen
Letter opener *(with your message engraved on it)*
Library lamp
Magnifying glass with light
Massaging chair or seat cushion
Monogrammed pencil cup
Mouse pad *(for his computer)*
Mug *(reproduce his business card on it)*
Multi-language translator
Neon sculpture
Paper shredder
Paperweight *(your picture in it)*
Pencil set
Pencil sharpener with personalized pencils
Pepper spray pen
Personal embosser
Personalized wall clock
Stamp holder
Stereo system
Stone sculpture
Unique wastepaper basket

CAR "TOYS"

- Aftershave
- Auto shop mats *(for his garage floor)*
- Beverage cooler
- Car alarm system
- Car cover *(elegant)*
- Car duster
- Car emergency kit
- Car mats
- Car phone holder
- Card holder for his business cards
- CD or cassette from his favorite show
- Drink holder
- Driving moccasins
- Electric vacuum that plugs into a cigarette lighter
- Eyeglass holder
- Flashlight *(for glove compartment)*
- Jumper cables
- Key tracker
- License plate frame
- Magnetic case for spare car keys *(very important)*
- Model kit of his favorite car
- Night driving glasses
- Panoramic view mirror
- Pepper spray key chain
- Precision meter to measure miles by the inch
- Radar detector
- Seat cover
- Sheepskin seat cover
- Sport sunglasses
- Steering wheel cover
- Sun shade protector
- Travel coffee maker

SPORT GIFTS

Aerobic machine
Autographed baseball
Autographed football
Bicycle
Billiard set
Boxing bag
Cholesterol tester
Fishing fly
Fishing set
Foot massager
Golf shirt
Golf bag
Golf book
Golf club ID cap
Golf club cover *(for each club)*
Health club membership
Inline skates *(with helmet)*
Jet ski
Karate lessons
Kinetic moped
Magazines
Monogrammed bowler's towel
Monogrammed golf balls
Monogrammed golf putting set
Personal scale if he is on a diet
Pinball game
Ping pong table
Pool table *(half size)*
Personal trainer for a week
Punching bag *(with gloves)*
Secret money sock
Shorts
Silver-plated barbells
Snow steppers *(winter workout)*
Snowboard
Sports bag
Sports sandals
Sport shoes *(with athletic socks)*
Sports equipment
Swimmer's radio
T-shirt
Tennis racket *(with personal trainer)*
Tennis table *(folding)*
Waterproof watch
Workout suit

"JUST BECAUSE" GIFTS

- Adjustable top table (*for eating in front of the TV*)
- Bagel Bakery
- Balloons
- Bathrobe
- Belt
- Birthday cards
- Book about fatherhood
- Book about his hobby (*most recent edition*)
- Bottle of wine with corkscrew
- Boxer shorts (seven) for each day of the week
- Breathe Rite nasal strip
- Cakes
- Cigar box for his jewelry
- Coffee/tea mug
- Cookies, heart-shaped (*with his name in frosting*)
- Cuff-links (*monogrammed*)
- Diet sweets in fancy box
- Dinner
- Flowers
- Footstool
- Handkerchiefs
- Harmonica mini-pendant
- Keychain
- Lap desk
- Musical instrument
- Personalized mug with his (*grand*) child's photo
- Photo puzzle
- Pie in the shape of a heart
- Pillow (*for reading and sitting*)
- Poster with his favorite movie star
- Professional massage
- Safari jacket
- Silk boxer shorts
- Socks with funny printing
- Book of solitaire games
- Tickets for a play or musical
- Tie case
- Toiletry bag
- Umbrella
- Videotapes (*his favorite movie star*)

FOR LOVERS AND OTHERS

Antique champagne glasses
  (*with champagne*)
Belt and tie rack
Blank book (*for a journal*)
Cashmere scarf
Celebrity tie collection
Collar for his dog
  (*with the dog's name on it*)
Compact disk collection
Customized street sign
Director's chair
Dress shirt
Dresser top organizer
Electric pants presser
Fabric book cover
Flannel robe
Gloves
Gold bracelet
Golden toothbrush
Jewelry box
Leather vest or jacket
Neck chain
New reading glasses
Personal groomer
Personal travel bags for his suits

Personalized coasters
Private safe
  (*know the combination*)
Professional massage
Reader's pillow
Religious symbols
  (*cross, mezuzah, etc.*)
Rocking chair
Seven-day pill holder
Sheepskin slippers
Silk lounge pants
Silk pillowcase
Silk robe (*Playboy, if possible*)
Silver-plated bottle stopper
  (*personalized*)
Special show box
Stamp collection with stamps
Tickets for his favorite musical
Towel stand (*heated*)
Travel journal
Travel wallet for passport, tickets, credit cards
Watch
Wind chime
Wine from his birth year

Chapter Ten

Finally!

❦ ❦ ❦

"How to Find a Bingo" will help you look for clues
on what to buy.

"Creative Presentations" gives scores of ways to wrap
and present your gifts.

Greeting card ideas and the invitation will make
his birthday more fun, while the advertising
won't cost you a dime!

Remember
It's not the gift—it's the presentation.
Little things mean a lot.

HOW TO FIND A "BINGO!"

FINALLY, YOU DECIDE to buy your partner a selection of gifts, but you have no idea what to get for him. Any time you are together, look and listen for a **"Bingo!"** What is a bingo?

A bingo is a clue into your partner's wants and desires. Here are some bingo examples.

If you are driving along in the car with the radio on, and your man says, "Oh, I really like this song," or starts singing along with it, Bingo! You have a gift idea (the CD or tape of that song).

Place books or catalogs of vacation getaways around the house and watch for his reaction. Bingo!

Casually tell him about a gift your friend has bought for her husband and see how he reacts. Bingo!

If you notice that when people ask for his phone number, he has to scribble it out on a piece of paper, Bingo! Get him some personal cards professionally printed.

All you have to do is watch, wait, and listen, and you will be sure to find a few Bingo's!

ADVICE

Make a Bingo list so you won't forget.

CREATIVE PRESENTATIONS

GIFT WRAPPING IS ALWAYS PART OF THE PRESENTATION. Here are some **unusual gift wrapping ideas.** Pick the one you like, add your imagination, and create your presentation.

Bandanna (*for small gifts*)
Basket
Bath towel
Beach towel
Bear on a brown bag with the words "I Love You"
Brass planter
Brown bag
Business card holder (*to hold small gift*)
Chinese food take out carton (*empty*)
Chocolate box (*empty*)
Cigar box
Comic strips
Computer printout (*put message on it to use as wrapping paper*)
Cookie box
Crystal candy dish
Decorate a lunch box

Decorate a shoe box
Dress the box with men's belts
Florist's box
Glue love card collage on blank paper or on the gift box
Heart-shaped stamps on white paper
Ice cream box (*empty*)
Jewelry box
Kitchen towel
"Love" stamps on plain paper
Lunch size paper bag
Map of his city or other map
Metal gallon container
Mixed nut box
Movie popcorn box (*cleaned*)
Newspaper pages from his favorite section
Oversized calendar page— put a "♥" on his birthday

Photocopied enlargement of his/your picture

Picnic basket

Pillow cases with your message written on them

Playboy, Time, Sport Illustrated pages or covers

Poster of his favorite movie or TV person

Road map

School box, good for pens, pencils, or small gifts

Sheet music of "your song"

Simple white paper that you write on

Simple wood box

Small mailbox with a personalized flag

Special toilet paper that reads "Happy Birthday"
(for small gifts)

Tablecloth

Tablecloth for larger gift with matching napkins for smaller gifts

Two different colors of wrapping paper
(ex: black and white)

VCR box
(especially good for gifts of tickets)

Velvet

Wastepaper basket

Wrap the gift like candy and tie each end with a ribbon

Wrap with a canvas rope

Write love words on a wide ribbon and use to wrap gifts

MANY BIRTHDAY CARDS

HAVE YOU EVER FOUND YOURSELF in a greeting card store unable to choose **just the right card** for your partner's birthday?

Solve this problem by buying all the cards that you like. Put all of the cards in a box and write on the box "Honestly, I liked them all," or "They all say what I feel about you," or "They all remind me of you."

You can present the box alone, or give it along with one of the ideas for multiple gifts in Chapter Seven.

OPTION

Another way to present all the cards is to make a small book out of them by punching two holes in the side of each card and tying them all together with ribbon.

CARDS, CARDS, CARDS

ON HIS BIRTHDAY, give your partner **one card for each year of his life.** You can give him the cards one day at a time or all at once. However, when you shop for these cards, don't buy the usual humorous type of birthday card. Buy only cards that say "I love you," or "To the love of my life," or that have romantic messages on them. These cards are sensitive and romantic, and will express more about closeness, love, and tenderness than other kinds of birthday cards.

OPTION

These cards can be useful as models when you want to create your own personal card.

INVITATION TO HIS PARTY

A GREAT WAY TO INVITE your partner to **his own surprise party** is to make a fake party invitation to a mutual friend's party.

Make the surprise party a week or more before his real birthday so he will not be suspicious. Ask him to participate and help with the pretend surprise party for his friend.

The personal invitations for him can be purchased at any party store and carefully mailed so he suspects nothing.

TIPS

Make sure your partner is absolutely certain this is his friend's surprise party.

Don't forget to notify all the guests about how the surprise is being carried out. Make sure the friend whose name you are using for the fake party knows your plans, too.

ADVERTISING

THERE ARE MANY WAYS to **advertise your partner's birthday** in the newspaper. If you would like to surprise him but don't like the idea of placing ads in the newspaper (or if you are on a tight budget), you can still use the newspaper to wish him a happy birthday.

Get the newspaper before he does and write "Happy Birthday" with a red marker on each page of the newspaper so that, when he reads it, he will see his very own birthday wish.

TIPS

If you prefer, you can place the "Happy Birthday" wish in his favorite newspaper section only.

When using the marker, do not cover up the articles he will want to read.

YOUR FAVORITE GIFT IDEAS

LIST HERE all of the gift ideas that appealed to you in this book. By writing them down, you will be able to locate them quickly when you need the perfect gift for your partner.

Gift Name	Occasion	Page #

Gift Name	Occasion	Page #

Afterword

AS YOU READ THIS BOOK, you may get some great gift ideas of your own or remember gifts you have given your partner in the past which were especially memorable or fun.

If you would like to share your ideas, please send them to me along with your name, address, and phone number. I will try to include your original gift idea, along with your name, in my next book.

Mail your gift ideas to:

> Haya Gil Lubin
> *Show Him Your Love*
> P.O. Box 80745
> Las Vegas, NV 89180-0745

> *Happy gift giving!*
> – Haya

ORDER FORM

For additional copies of
Show Him Your Love, More Than 101 Gift Ideas for the Man in Your Life, call:

1-800-594-5190
(MASTERCARD AND VISA ACCEPTED)

or fill out the order form below.

Send me _____ copies of *Show Him Your Love, More Than 101 Gift Ideas for the Man in Your Life* at $12.95 per book plus $3.50 postage and handling.

NAME _____

ADDRESS _____

CITY/STATE/ZIP _____

DAYTIME PHONE _____

    $12.95 per book $ _____
    $3.50 shipping (one book) $ _____
    $1.00 shipping for each additional book $ _____
    Total $ _____

☐ Check enclosed

☐ Charge my: ☐ Mastercard   ☐ Visa

    NUMBER _____ EXP. DATE _____

    SIGNATURE _____

Mail to: Chicago Spectrum Press • 1571 Sherman Ave • Annex C • Evanston, IL 60201 (Fax: 847-492-1967)